Friends United

Mary Green

Folens

United Kingdom: Folens Publishers, Apex Business Centre, Boscombe Road, Dunstable, LU5 4RL.
Email: folens@folens.com

Ireland: Folens Publishers, Greenhills Road, Tallaght, Dublin 24.
Email: info@folens.ie

Poland: JUKA, ul. Renesansowa 38, Warsaw 01-905.

Editor: Kay Macmullan
Layout artist: Suzanne Ward
Cover design: John Hawkins
Illustrations: Josephine Blake

First published 2004 by Folens Limited.

British Library Cataloguing in Publication Data. A catalogue record for this publication is available from the British Library.

ISBN 1 84303 684–3

Contents

The story so far

If you haven't read an *On the edge* book before:
The stories take place in and around a row of shops and buildings called Pier Parade in Brightsea, right next to the sea. There's Big Fry, the fish and chip shop; Drop Zone, the drop-in centre for local teenagers; Macmillan's, the sweet and souvenir shop; Anglers' Haven, the fishing tackle shop; the Surf 'n' Skate shop and, of course, the Brightsea Beach Bar.

If you have read an *On the edge* book you may have met some of these people before.

Sam Roberts:	*lives with his mum and dad, and older brother, David. They have just moved into the Brightsea area.*
Greg Davy:	*lives with his grandfather, Charlie, who owns and runs Anglers' Haven, the fishing shop.*

So, what's been going on?
Greg finds it hard to mix with the tougher boys at school, and has no older brother or sister to look after him. Sam is new to the area, and is keen to settle in and be accepted. He's clever, and quite cool, but that doesn't guarantee friendships.

What happens in this story?
Sam arrives for his first day at his new school and immediately comes across Mark, who takes an instant dislike to him. Greg watches what happens, and when the chance comes, tries to strike up a friendship with Sam.

1

Being new

Sam walked up the path.

His bag was heavy.

It was new.

His shirt was new as well.

Everything about him was new.

He walked through the school gates.

Some kids were looking at him.

He turned to them.

They looked away.

He went into his new classroom.

The teacher was asking the class to sit still.

“This is Sam Roberts,” he said.

“I want you all to welcome him.

It’s his first day.”

No one smiled.

No one said a word.

No one did anything.

Sam felt like the new boy.

He sat down and looked out of the window.

Sam felt like the new boy.

Sam spent all morning looking out of the window.

He didn't want to speak to anyone.

He didn't like this new school.

It wasn't friendly.

When lunch came he sat on his own.

Then he walked around.

Some girls talked to him.

He didn't know what to say.

So they left.

But they pulled at his new bag and laughed at him first.

They pulled at his new bag and laughed at him.

When Sam got home he went into the kitchen.

"How were things today?" asked his dad. "Made any friends yet?"

"Yeah," said Sam. "Loads."

The door opened.

David, his older brother, came in.

He had a new friend from college with him.

It was clear David was doing just fine.

"Golden boy," said Sam to himself as he went up to his room.

2

History lesson

Sam was in a History lesson.

He liked History.

Mr Patel was the teacher.

"I see we've got a good student here," said Mr Patel.

One of the boys at the back made a rude noise.

Mr Patel looked at him.

The noise stopped.

The bell went.

Mr Patel left and Sam got up to leave too.

But the boy from the back of the class stood in his way.

He was with two mates.

"Who's a clever boy, then?" he said in a silly voice.

Everyone stopped.

Perhaps there would be a punch-up.

Sam stood still.

He didn't get angry.

He stayed cool.

Who's a clever boy, then?

"What's wrong with doing some work?" said Sam.

The boy made a face.

Sam stepped forward.

"What's wrong with it, then?" said Sam. "Go on. Tell me. If you can, that is."

It was the way Sam said it.

He could have been saying, "Don't mess with me, if you know what's good for you."

What's wrong with doing some work?

Sam looked at the crowd of kids.

"He can't tell me, can he?" he said to them.

"Come on, Mark," said a kid. "You don't know, do you?"

"Get lost!" said Mark.

Sam walked towards the door.

Mark didn't stop him.

He just stood there.

One of the kids in the class shouted out, "Own goal, Mark!"

3

Mark can't win

It was break.

Sam was kicking his football around in the playground.

Suddenly Mark was next to him.

He was with his two mates.

Before Sam knew it, Mark had the ball.

He kicked it to one of his mates.

The three boys kept passing the ball between them.

They were trying to make Sam mad.

But Sam did nothing.

He leaned against the wall.

Then Mark kicked the ball hard into the long grass.

That was it.

The ball had gone.

Sam walked away.

He looked as if he didn't care.

But Mark came after him.

He hit Sam in the back.

Mark kicked the ball hard into the long grass.

Sam turned round, slowly.

He faced Mark.

Then he gave him such a look that Mark stepped back.

"Leave off," said one of Mark's mates.

He knew Mark couldn't win.

It was clear.

Sam was no push-over.

"Yeah," said Mark lamely. "Come on. He's a waste of time."

They all walked off.

Sam knew that Mark wouldn't bother him again.

Sam knew that Mark wouldn't bother him again.

Greg Davy also knew what Sam was like.

Everyone was talking about him.

How he'd faced up to Mark.

How he didn't care what other kids said.

But so far Greg had kept out of it all.

He liked a quiet life.

Now he was holding Sam's football.

He had seen Mark kick it.

It had landed at Greg's feet.

4

Meeting Greg

Sam was fed up.

Mark was off his back.

It was true.

The lessons were OK.

Most of them anyway.

But he still had no friends.

"I don't want any," he said to himself.

"Not in this place. It stinks."

So when Greg came up to him, Sam said nothing.

Greg opened his bag.

He took out Sam's football.

"Here, man. I think this is yours," said Greg.

"Where did you find that?' asked Sam.

Greg told him how the football had found him.

"Thanks," said Sam. "I owe you."

"No you don't," said Greg. "Anyone would do it."

"Not in this place," said Sam and he got up and walked off.

Here, man. I think this is yours.

It was lunchtime.

There was a long line.

Greg was waiting to be served.

The dinner lady was putting food on his plate.

Then Mark pushed in.

"Get back," he said. "This is my place."

He dug Greg in the arm.

The plate crashed to the ground.

The food went everywhere.

The dinner lady stopped.

She came round to have a look.

The food went everywhere.

"You'll have to pay for it," she said to Greg.

"What?" asked Greg.

"If you mess about you have to pay."

"I didn't do it!"

"Well, who did then?" she asked.

Greg looked round.

Mark had gone.

"Well, someone will have to pay for it," she said. "And it looks like it's going to be you."

5

Making friends

Sam was watching Greg.

A teacher was talking to him.

He was saying Greg had to pay.

"That Mark is a real pain," Sam said to himself.

He felt sorry for Greg.

He had no money left to buy more food.

Sam went over to him.

"Have some of my packed lunch," he said. "Remember, I owe you."

Greg laughed.

They shared the packed lunch and chatted.

They had a lot in common.

The bell went for the end of lunch.

"Want a quick game after school?" asked Sam.

Greg wasn't much good at football but he liked Sam.

"There's a pitch near the gym," he replied.

They shared the packed lunch and chatted.

It was a good pitch.

Sam felt happy.

He played really well and scored two goals.

Others from the class joined in.

When it was over, everyone patted Sam on the back.

"You're a good player," said someone.

"Skilful," said one of the girls.

"Hi, Sam," said another.

She gave him a beaming smile.

You're a good player.

When Sam got home, David was making a pot of tea in the kitchen.

He poured a cup for Sam and handed it to him.

"Here you are, little bro," he said.

For once, Sam didn't reply.

Instead he smiled.

"You're in a good mood," said David.

Sam's dad was there too.

He stopped reading his newspaper.

He looked at Sam.

"How were things today?" he asked.

"Made any friends yet?"

Glossary

beaming smile	wide, happy smile
bro	shortened form of brother
(to) face up to (someone)	(to) stand up to (someone)
fed up	unhappy, depressed
golden boy	someone who gets all the luck and attention
lamely	without effect
loads	lots, many
(to) mess with (someone)	(to) try to cause trouble with (someone)
(to get) off someone's back	(to) stop bothering someone
own goal	goal scored in your own net (giving points to your opponent)
packed lunch	cold lunch brought to school
punch-up	fight
push-over	someone who is easily beaten